FORGIVENESS

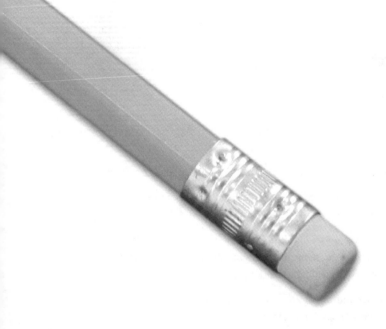

RON KALLMIER

CONTENTS

INTRODUCTION

◎ IS FORGIVENESS 'A BRIDGE TOO FAR'?

On more than one occasion in His teaching, Jesus emphasised how important it is to God that we have a forgiving attitude to others.

Which is fine in theory, but …

Each one of us, with a few moments' reflection, can recall the words or actions of others that have harmed us physically, emotionally or spiritually. These are part of the rough and tumble of everyday life in a fallen world. Some of these events are minor and we can negotiate our way past them. Others carry sufficient sting to affect us considerably – even throughout our lives.

Unhappily, there are many people who have endured short-term and long-term emotional and physical damage at the whim of others. Often these experiences have transformed the victim's thinking and personality.

As you read the words above, examples may now be going through your mind from your own experience.

And then, of course, there are those who have been the offenders and find they cannot forgive themselves, and so live their lives enshrouded with guilt and guilt feelings.

For some the journey across the bridge of forgiveness is short. For others it may take months or years. There is an optimum time when God begins to nudge us to confront forgiveness issues. True wisdom is involved in discerning this time and taking the opportunity for the greater freedom that forgiveness provides.

This book is written in the firm belief that forgiveness is an important element of personal wellbeing. It may be used individually or in a supportive small group. It is designed to help you explore important biblical teaching on the subject and to address the practical matters involved in forgiving and being forgiven. The issues covered include:

- How can a person forgive in certain circumstances?
- Is forgiveness unrealistic?
- What should we do when we feel unable to forgive?
- Is there a practical way to forgive someone who has hurt us so badly?
- What if it has not stopped?
- What if we realise that we have caused harm to others?

HOW TO USE THIS BOOK

There are seasons in each of our lives when the issue of hurt, pain and the need for forgiveness surfaces. This book has been prepared to offer suggestions for such seasons. You can work through this book either on your own or in a group setting. The choice is yours.

May you have safe passage across the bridge of forgiveness!

◎ SUGGESTIONS FOR YOUR PERSONAL USE OF THIS BOOK

- The book is divided into four sessions. Read the content and the associated scriptures at your own pace.
- You may find it helpful to have a journal at hand. You may choose to record insights and questions, specific issues and decisions you make along the way.
- There are two extra sections containing very practical suggestions on the process of forgiving and being forgiven. Try to work through them and put them into practice.
- You may prefer to work through these practical steps with a trusted friend.

◎ SUGGESTIONS FOR GROUPS WHO USE THIS BOOK

Although this study is intended as a four-week course, there is additional material that could extend this to six weeks.

1) Using the book over four group meetings

If you plan to use the book in this way, it is recommended that group members be encouraged to pre-read all the relevant notes, reflections and meditations to be used in the following group meeting.

You may choose to follow a meeting-to-meeting plan such as this:

Week 1 – Beginnings

Week 2 – The Power to Choose

To prepare for Week 3, encourage group members to work through the practical steps on pages 21–24, entitled 'Practical suggestions when forgiving an offender'.

Week 3 – Responding wisely
To prepare for Week 4, encourage group members to work through the practical steps on pages 31–33 entitled 'Finding forgiveness when I am the offender'.
Week 4 – Overcoming

2) Using this book over six group meetings
If you feel the material on pages 21–24 and 31–33 would be suitable for group use rather than just individual reflection, then you could use the two sections as Weeks 3 and 5.

NOTES FOR GROUP LEADERS

- This book has both a biblical focus and a practical focus. You may choose either or both approaches. The included quotes may be a starting point for group discussion.
- The intention in writing this book has been to give options for each group in planning its own preferred pathway through the topic.
- It is recommended that groups address real issues from within the group as far as is appropriate.
- As you share in your groups, be aware that this topic is potentially both painful and liberating for those who struggle with the issue of forgiveness. Since each group and every member is different, it is recommended that you stop, share and pray whenever the group believes this is necessary. Proceed at a pace that the group members agree is realistic.
- An agreement of confidentiality may be important to some members in your group.
- Please do not pressure anyone to share when they are unwilling.
- For those persons who find the issues of forgiveness particularly difficult, personal follow-up is recommended, either by friends, a pastor, pastoral carers, prayer team members or counsellors. For some, an experienced counsellor or therapist may be required.
- Feel free to use what is helpful, to ignore the remainder, or to add your own ideas.
- *Group leaders are strongly advised to check that all members are in a satisfactory emotional and spiritual place at the end of each session.*

May you and your group understand and experience the freedom of forgiveness in deeper ways.

Ron Kallmier

GETTING STARTED

Do you remember, as a child, sitting in the family car with your brothers or sisters, preparing for a long journey? Remember how cramped the back seat space appeared to be? And your brother or sister always took up too much space when you were trying to get comfortable!

After a while, pushing became hitting and then shouting, until your parents intervened from the front seat, telling you to 'Stop hitting, _____, and say you are sorry.'

'But he (or she) started it!' you replied. And the journey continued with glares and pulled faces, while the pushing became more subtle.

Even as children, we humans find it difficult to own up to our faults and not to hold grudges. On more serious issues, genuine forgiveness is not natural to us and does not come easily.

- Perhaps this is, in part, because we believe that by forgiving someone else we make what was done to us seem unimportant.
- Perhaps our anger at the injustice done to us is the cause.
- Perhaps it is simply because we view our world and the events that occur around us from our point of view only.
- Perhaps we are still too close to the pain of the offence.
- Or perhaps we see forgiveness as letting the offender off too lightly.

In the Old Testament culture of Israel (as well as some surrounding cultures) the Law of Tallion was used – the principle of an eye for an eye, a tooth for a tooth, an animal for an animal, a life for a life. There is a certain natural justice in this approach. Harm done was paid for in the same kind. In fact, the law was a way of limiting revenge and preventing over-reaction. It appeared fair and just, but it had its limitations. While it did not rule out mercy, it did not encourage it either.

Mahatma Gandhi made quite an insightful comment when he said,

If we practise an eye for an eye and a tooth for a tooth, soon the whole world will be blind and toothless.

Additionally, revenge damages our souls. This damage is unavoidable, even when the revenge appears justified to us, and even if the offence was illegal. The problem is that revenge uncovers a heart attitude that says, 'I want to hurt you because you hurt me.'

In fact, what we do by retaliating is give permission for the offender to bring us into their 'game' and to play by their rules. Their game plan traps us by distracting us from who we really are and what we truly want to be doing in our lives. We may miss the high calling that God has for each of us. Our thoughts, attitudes and behaviour become entangled and distorted in the process. How many lives have become bitter and twisted by the reaction to the words and actions of others!

The teaching of Jesus emphasises a healthier, better way for all concerned. It flows out of a heart that is responsive. It is characterised by forgiveness and blessing. The Old Testament Law, like our laws today, dealt with the externals of life – how we should *act*. Jesus, on the other hand, focused on what was happening in *the heart* – the control centre of our personality. The Sermon on the Mount (Matt. 5–7) is essentially about the human heart. Many years earlier the book of Proverbs paved the way for this revelation: 'Above all else, guard your heart, for it is the wellspring of life' (Prov. 4:23).

Jesus' teaching raised the understanding of God's expectation of us to a whole new level (see, for example, Matt. 5:43–48). This high expectation is possibly one reason why forgiveness is so hard for us. In fact, as we discover from personal experience, we can only live as Jesus intended us to live by the power of the Holy Spirit – one of the reasons He came to us at Pentecost. He is our source of direction and power as we confront the demons of the offences done to us – and those offences we have committed ourselves.

As we begin the journey across the bridge of forgiveness, it is good to examine our hearts before God. Take some time to be still in His presence and invite Him to show you the answers to the following three questions:

- Is there any person or offence that you find difficult to forgive?
- Are you harbouring bitter, vengeful thoughts towards another individual or group?

- Is God putting His finger on anything in your life for which you need to be forgiven?

◎ PRAYER OF PREPARATION

Psalm 139
My heavenly Father, I thank You that You have always known everything there is to know about me, and that You have never ceased loving me. I take the words of David for myself as I seek to cross the bridge of forgiveness:

Search me, O God, and know my heart;
test me and know my anxious thoughts.
See if there is any offensive way in me,
and lead me in the way everlasting.
                                    Psa. 139:23–24

BEGINNINGS

Focal Passage: Matthew 18:15–35

◎ 1. TO WALK IN JESUS' STEPS

Luke 23:26–35

I find it quite difficult to read the story of the suffering and crucifixion of our Lord Jesus Christ. This is partly because my imagination becomes engaged in the pain and injustice of it all. But no matter how hard I try, I cannot picture how He could have hung on a cross and offered forgiveness to those who, in ignorance, were nailing Him, the Son of God, to that tree. This is extreme forgiveness – hanging there on a cross, forgiving His murderers, and opening up the possibility of forgiveness and new life to the whole world.

Notice how Jesus stayed in control throughout the mockery of the trial, the beatings and the cross itself. Perhaps it was the fact that He did not curse His tormentors or cry out vengeful words that so impressed the guards, even before the heavens split and raged.

His ministry years are full of episodes of forgiveness and new beginnings. In the Gospel accounts we see Jesus addressing individuals and their specific guilt: a man lowered through a broken roof, a woman thrown at His feet.

So it was not only in His teaching, but also in His dying, that Jesus underscored the principle and practice of forgiveness. And this message was communicated to His disciples; for example, the martyr, Stephen, understood the importance of forgiveness even at the point of his own death (Acts 7, especially verses 54–60, see below).

Reflection on the Scriptures
Acts 7:54–60
- Spend a few moments reading these verses. Think about the event from Stephen's point of view.
- What was the key thing that motivated Stephen to respond as he did?
- What does this teach us?

For meditation and discussion
- If you were to die tomorrow, would there be any lack of forgiveness in your heart towards a person who had wronged you?
- Would you have any regrets about this situation?

2. TO OPEN THE WAY TO RECEIVE FORGIVENESS FOR OURSELVES

Matthew 18:15–22

The apostle Paul reminded us: '… for all have sinned and fall short [miss the mark] of the glory of God' (Rom. 3:23). At some time and in some way we are all guilty of offences against God and against others. We need to be forgiving as much as we need to be forgiven.

Forgiveness of others displays the true state of our heart. It recognises that God is a forgiving God and that He desires us to follow after His example.

Those of us who are secure or scarred or struggling will approach forgiveness from different starting points:

- The secure may forgive because they understand that they gain nothing from holding onto a grudge.
- The scarred may forgive because they have fought and won some significant, tough life battles. Wounds have occurred but healing is also in process. From their experiences, they have come to understand the true significance of forgiveness for their own wellbeing.
- The struggling may forgive because they weigh the prospects of forgiveness against their tendency to wallow in their own pain. They recognise that forgiveness is not too high a price to pay for their release from the pain of the past.

Reflection on the Scriptures

Ephesians 4:32

The message in Matthew 18:15–22 is quite clear and profoundly challenging.

- What appears to be the most surprising statement?
- What is the most difficult part of this teaching to accept?

For meditation and discussion

- Many of us have faced the reality of having to forgive individuals on more than one occasion. What is the main point that Jesus is making here?
- Does forgiving include being reconciled and trusting the offender again?

THE POWER
TO CHOOSE

◎ 1. TO LIFT THE BURDEN OF THE OFFENCE

Philippians 4

When someone has offended us we 'carry the load' of that offence until a positive act of resolution, such as forgiveness, is completed. It is like having a ball and chain attached to us. We can still move around but the offence handicaps us and we are continually conscious of it. Other offences will add to it.

Forgiveness is the central way to restore personal inner wholeness. We take control of the situation that was imposed upon us. We cut it off through the act of forgiveness. We declare that it will no longer hinder our lives.

It is vital though to recognise that, simply because we have made the hard choice to forgive, the pain will not necessarily diminish immediately. Nor does it mean that we will never be hurt again by the same person(s). Further, the emotionally scarred areas of our life often remain very sensitive to similar offences. It is in circumstances like these that we need to draw on the wisdom and empowerment of the Holy Spirit, and the support and encouragement of friends, to pursue the freedom that forgiveness offers. Remember that forgiveness is a journey more than a destination.

It is important to add that forgiving does not require us to become a 'doormat' for others to walk over, but our actions should be consistent with the heart and lifestyle of Jesus Christ.

Reflection on the Scriptures

Hebrews 4:14–16

- Take time to bring to Jesus any offences against you that continue to cause you concern. He is willing to provide mercy and grace (strength) in your times of need.

For meditation and discussion

Offences vary in how long the damaging actions have continued and how severe the impact is on us. For some extreme and particularly damaging offences, we may need the guidance and support of mature, wise friends to help us through.

The gentle 'nudging' of the Holy Spirit to forgive someone is a helpful indicator that it is time to take this journey towards forgiveness seriously. Consider the following:

- As you have been reading and thinking about this topic, have past hurts come to mind that need to be faced or have you become aware of people who need your forgiveness?
- Are you in a place where you want to move on, to forgive, to be free of it?

⊚ 2. TO RECOGNISE THAT THE PAST CANNOT BE CHANGED

Forgiveness is giving up the possibility of a better past. Mike D.

Reflecting on earlier setbacks in our lives, it is not uncommon for us to dream about what could have been or should have been. One way in which we can recognise that we are beginning to move on is when we accept that the past is truly *past*. It can never be changed. It is out of reach. What happened, happened, whether we liked it or not.

As obvious as this may appear, many people spend countless hours chewing over the ideal script for their past lives; how the pain they experienced could have been avoided, and the good dreams they cherished fulfilled. But this is a dead end. It can begin a cycle of regretful thoughts that go nowhere and may result in depression or despair.

Harm from other people often leaves lasting emotional scars on us. While the event itself may have been very hurtful, in fact, the way we think about it may do us greater long-term harm.

The hurtful event may be tossed around in our minds and examined from various points of view, over and over again. The event does not change, but our thinking about it does change us! It is common for a person's view of self to be diminished or robbed by the thoughts they have following the offence.

If such events occur when we are children, it is most unhelpful to consider better ways in which we could have responded. Often it is the adult's ways, not the child's ways that we envisage. In counselling situations it is not uncommon to hear comments from formerly wounded children like the following:

- 'I should have stopped it.'
- 'I should have stood up for my rights.'
- 'I should have just walked away.'
- 'Why didn't I just say …?'

The reason for such comments is that, as adults, we forget how a child experiences and responds to these situations in his/her world. In retrospect, we put adult thoughts and actions upon the younger version of ourselves.

As for the adult, so for the wounded child. The past is past!

Reflection on the Scriptures

Philippians 3:12–16; 2 Corinthians 11:16–12:10

Paul had been through all the tests imaginable and had found the secret of coming out strong on the other side. While the texts focus on his physical wellbeing, it is clear that he applied the same principles to all of his life (2 Cor. 12:10).

For meditation and discussion

When you hear an older person talking about 'the good old days' do you find that often you are somewhat cynical? Were the good old days really so good? For some, undoubtedly yes. For many of us, our amazing minds selectively remember things. Some people dwell only on the positives. Others dwell on the negatives. Some manage a better balance.

Whether it was especially good or painfully difficult, the past is over. We cannot reach back into it and make any difference. The future does not yet exist, though we may influence its shape in the present.

We have today – only today!

- Generally speaking, are you a forward-looking or backward-looking person?
- Do you plan to use today to dwell on the past with its regrets and unfulfilled possibilities?
- Do you plan to use today to do everything you can to ensure that the negative experiences of the past do not continue to be a snare for your future?

3. TO PLACE A 'LINE IN THE SAND' IN RELATION TO THE EVENT

Offering forgiveness to another is a way of saying, 'I am not allowing this offence to dominate my life and my thoughts any longer. I make a choice that it ends here and it ends with forgiveness.'

It is important to realise that this is a *choice*. If we wait until we *feel* ready to do it, the time may never arrive. Sometimes this decision has to be taken with gritted teeth. It will be contested internally, and the behaviour of other people around us may not encourage us either. And there is often the nagging whisper of the enemy encouraging us to keep on hating, or affirming our right to remain angry.

The decision to forgive is so difficult, but the benefits are surprising. They touch us spiritually, emotionally, relationally and rationally.

- Spiritually, we learn to walk in the ways of our Master and Friend, and so to explore something of what it means to live life to its fullest (John 10:10).
- Emotionally, we begin to live in a new way, no longer controlled by feelings of powerlessness.
- Relationally, our demeanour around others is more positive.
- Rationally, we reclaim our rights to think positive thoughts, to dream and hope better things for the future, and to celebrate our true identity as God intended.

Greater freedom awaits us as we continue our journey across 'forgiveness bridge'.

When you hold resentment toward another, you are bound to that person or condition by an emotional link that is stronger than steel. Forgiveness is the only way to dissolve that link and get free. Catherine Ponder

Reflection on the Scriptures
Psalm 103; Hebrews 10:15–18; Jeremiah 31:31–34
While there is no need for us to pay the price of forgiveness that Jesus did, we can learn much from His forgiving attitude to His flawed and failing people. Especially, we can learn how He draws His 'line in the sand' over our offences!

- Spend a few moments jotting down the key qualities of a forgiving heart as described in these Scriptures.
- You may add some thoughts from other biblical references if you choose.

For meditation and discussion

Carry out a simple self-check:

- Has any offence against me from the past diminished my relationship with God and my value of myself as a human being?
- Have my feelings become more depressing or angry since I suffered the offence?
- Has my thought life since the event(s) tended towards pessimism, vengeance or negativity?
- Has my personality been altered in some negative way as a consequence of one or more specific offences committed against me?
- How can I place my 'line in the sand' in regard to this troubling offence or offences?

The following material can be used either as **preparation for Week 3**, or, should your group be taking six weeks over this study, as **Week 3.**

PRACTICAL SUGGESTIONS WHEN FORGIVING AN OFFENDER

STEP 1: Be convinced that God is a loving, forgiving God

- Are you confident that God loves you and has a forgiving attitude towards you?
  This is important because forgiveness, being difficult, will require His involvement and empowerment.

STEP 2: Clarify the particular offence(s) against you by this individual (or group)

- This is when you can 'own' in detail what actually occurred and how it affected you.
- Make a suitable time and place available in order to reflect on the offence(s), perhaps with a trusted confidant if the offence is a major influence in your life.
- This ownership may only be in your mind but you will find that it proves very powerful to speak it out also. To confess the offence(s) with words and to hear what you say brings clarity as well as a sense of ownership.
- Be very specific. What was/were the offence(s) and how has it/have they impacted your life?

STEP 3: Seek to understand the motive behind the offence(s)

- Was it accidental? Do you believe that the person did not really intend to hurt you?
- Was the offence malicious? Did the person set out to really damage you mentally, physically, spiritually or emotionally?
- Was the offence ongoing (occurring more than once and/or over a period of time)?
- Did you do something previously to cause this offence to take place?

- Is the offender aware that what he/she did was so hurtful to you?
- Do you know why the offence happened?
- Is this offence still occurring? (If so and you sense being trapped by this, seek help from another trusted person before going any further with this book.)

STEP 4: Understanding the impact of the offence

- In what ways have you changed as a result of what was done to you?
- How much of this change has been caused by the way you have dwelt on the hurtful events in your mind?
- What is your attitude to the offender now?
- Are you aware of anger, bitterness, thoughts of revenge, depression or other unhelpful thoughts or emotions?
- Why are you considering forgiveness now?
- Forgiveness involves facing the pain of the offence and moving past it. Are you prepared for this?

STEP 5: Seek a divine perspective

- After you have worked through the steps above, wait on God for His insight into the offence and its effects. Do not rush ahead. Seek His help and wisdom.
- Meditation on relevant scriptures may prove insightful.
- God's perspective may be different from your human point of view.
- The support and wisdom of a trusted friend may be helpful to you at this point. Often God uses others to speak to His children.

STEP 6: Releasing forgiveness

- Invite the Holy Spirit to give insight and empowerment as to how He wants you to proceed with forgiveness. Speaking it out will be part of it, but should you be alone for this? Do you need to be heard by someone you trust? Should the offender hear? Is a letter or email required? Should you buy a gift? And so on …
- As you sense that the timing for forgiving is right for you, you may begin to feel intense emotional pain. If so, you will need to choose not to allow this pain to prevent you from moving towards forgiving.
- The choice to forgive begins by naming the offences and the offender before God (preferably out loud).
- As a deliberate act of will, speak forgiveness towards the other person out loud. Remember, this is a *choice* not just a desire. Here is a suggestion:

Heavenly Father, I *choose* to forgive _____(name) for _____ (the offence/s). I ask you to release him/her from the guilt of what he/she did to me. Please heal me from the effects of that offence on my life. In Jesus' name. Amen.

(Guard against the temptation to water your prayer down so that it goes something like this: 'Lord Jesus *help me* to forgive ….' or, 'God, I *want to* forgive …'. This is a definite choice you are making, now.)

- Pray, offering forgiveness, seeking God's healing and asking for His blessing on the person who has been forgiven, if he/she is still living. Speaking out your forgiveness is important whether the offender is still living or not.

STEP 7: Reconciliation and rebuilding trust

- Your act of forgiveness should only be discussed with the offender if he/she is aware of their offence and accepts their part in causing the problem. For this to be meaningful to the offender, it will be important for you to acknowledge any fault of your own if this is relevant.
- If you confront the offender and he/she had no knowledge of the offence nor any intent to harm you, your forgiveness will be an unhelpful surprise. It may cause the offender unnecessary problems just as you are finding your own freedom.

As a rule of thumb, if the offender is unaware of the offence and had no malice towards you in what he/she did, then simply share your forgiveness with a trusted independent party only. Deep forgiveness does not lose sight of the benefit it may bring to the offender.

- When we have been offended and the other party owns his/her error, reconciliation is possible. Recognise that reconciliation is an offer that you may choose to pursue. Reconciliation may never be appropriate, for example, in cases of physical or sexual abuse.
- Re-establishing trust is a deeper and much more difficult level of relational healing. It may never occur, but when it does, trust will be rebuilt slowly over a period of time.

Emotions and forgiveness arising from major offences against you

People who have followed a process such as the one suggested above have experienced immediate and significant positive impact. Interestingly, whether they are committed Christians or not appears to be irrelevant. There is a divine principle for human living involved here.

Nevertheless, it is important to be aware that each person's journey towards wholeness is different. For some it is relatively smooth and progressive. For others it is a battle of ongoing commitment to forgive until the pain eases.

Where the offence has been intensely damaging and also enduring, the timing of God and the wisdom of His Spirit as to the most appropriate way forward must be taken into account. This is not a situation where one approach suits everyone, though forgiveness is a life-giving and desirable goal for all.

Generally, it is advisable to deal with forgiveness matters as soon as possible. It is important that we realise that, in God's economy, there may be other priorities, other preparations required before this can take place successfully. Whatever the process or the timing, do not ignore the prompting of God's Holy Spirit. He knows the best time to forgive for each one of us.

It must be recognised also that forgiveness flies in the face of our normal human reactions to offences. Without God's help it may appear an unfair and unattractive option. This is not an easy path but it is a way to freedom once the end has been reached.

Forgiveness is rarely a straight-line affair, where we make a choice to forgive and that is that. It is more like a spiral upwards, where we keep touching the same or similar pain but gradually begin to think and act in a more forgiving, more released manner. This is the process of healing.

WEEK THREE
RESPONDING
WISELY

◎ **1. TO CUT SHORT THE PROSPECT OF FURTHER DAMAGE THROUGH REVENGE AND RETALIATION (EXTERNAL RESPONSE) OR VENGEFUL THINKING AND BITTERNESS (INTERNAL RESPONSE)**

The truth is, revenge can never restore what has been lost through the offences of another person. There may be a momentary feeling of satisfaction, but the root damage has not been addressed or undone. Revenge can never achieve that! Usually retaliation simply adds our own guilt to the guilt of the person who offended us. The problem is now compounded – and the effects are now much worse.

I remember once catching the last few minutes of a movie. The scene was in a dimly lit park among trees. On the ground was the still figure of a man. Standing over him was a man holding a smoking revolver, still pointed at the victim. What was stamped in my memory was his cry as the movie ended: 'How come I don't feel any better?'

What a telling example of the impotence of revenge to put things right. Daily on the TV news we watch both individuals and nations adding the weight of their testimony to the downward spiral caused by offences and revenge.

The following is a quote that is used frequently to illustrate the destructive force of revenge:

Revenge is like drinking poison and expecting the other person to die.

Anon

The writer of the letter to the Hebrews provides a most relevant correction by writing,

Make every effort to live in peace with all men and to be holy; without holiness no-one will see the Lord. See to it that no-one misses the grace of God and that no bitter root grows up to cause trouble and defile many.

Heb. 12:14–15

Bitterness is never self-contained, it always spills over to others, but the greatest damage is always to ourselves.

Reflection on the Scriptures
Hebrews 12:14–15

- Can you recall the faces of people who have ignored this piece of wisdom, and who are growing bitter within themselves and spilling the poisonous effects over onto others?
- Do you remember any real-life situations that are similar to the experience of the unforgiving servant (Matt. 18:21–35)?

For meditation and discussion

- Are you aware of people whose failure to forgive others has caused further damage to their own lives as a consequence?

- Have you ever found that you have grown bitter and hard-hearted because you have harboured a grudge against someone?
- How did this affect your life?
- How did you resolve that attitude and that grudge?

◎ 2. TO RESPOND IN THE OPPOSITE SPIRIT TO THE OFFENCE

Then Peter came to Jesus and asked, 'Lord, how many times shall I forgive my brother when he sins against me? Up to seven times?' Jesus answered, 'I tell you, not seven times, but seventy-seven times.' Matt. 18:21–22

Jesus' teaching in Romans 12:14–21 requires the inner working of the Holy Spirit to apply it in its fullest. Its instructions run contrary to every human desire for justice and revenge. As Paul penned these words towards the end of his life, he was not simply following some theoretical prompting from the Holy Spirit. The ministry years of his life were rich in examples where he had been through traumatic experiences and had found the liberating freedom of responding in the opposite manner to the offence.

Responding in the opposite spirit involves a painful choice and gritted-teeth action in many circumstances.

For Corrie Ten Boom, author of *The Hiding Place*,[1] it was confronting a former German guard from the concentration camp where her sister died and where she had suffered greatly. After an intense struggle, she released the power of forgiveness.

Forgiveness flies in the face of conventional wisdom, which is to get even, square off, pay back and so on. For many, the act of forgiveness may be perceived as a sign of weakness. For others, it may be considered to be an indicator of personal powerlessness.

Neither of these views is accurate. Forgiveness is tough. It is not for the faint-hearted. It requires facing squarely the offence and the offender (at least in the mind) and making the hard choice. There will be emotional pain involved to a greater or lesser degree. However, the benefits of the blessing from God and the freedom and peace that follow are worth it.

Reflection on the Scriptures

Romans 12:14–21

One of the great examples of forgiveness in the Old Testament period is the story of Joseph. Hated by his brothers, sold by them as a slave, falsely accused of attempted rape, forgotten in prison, Joseph had every reason to hate various people, become bitter and plot revenge.

When God promoted him to the position of second in command in Egypt he did not use his power to destroy his brothers when they finally discovered who he had become. He wept for them and blessed them (Gen. 50:15–21).

- What impresses you most about Joseph's attitude and behaviour?
- If you had been in his situation, what would you have done?

For meditation and discussion

- From your personal experience, what is it in your thinking that makes forgiveness so difficult for you?
- Are you facing a 'bridge' of forgiveness right now? What do you plan to do about it?

 3. TO BREAK THE POWER OF THE OFFENCE TO DEFINE WHO YOU ARE AND WHAT YOU MAY BECOME IN THE FUTURE

Suppose some significant adult (parent or teacher) says to us when we are young, 'You're hopeless! You'll never amount to anything!'

If this comment is taken seriously, there are two broadly dangerous routes we can travel down as a result:

- To prove the person wrong
- To receive it and believe it

In both cases, the negative words of another person are shaping our future.

The opinions of others, especially those with powerful influence in our lives, will have an impact on us. So what should we do?

- Check out if there *is* any truth in what was said. We do this by reflecting on the *integrity* of the person who spoke and the degree of their *commitment to our wellbeing*. How *reliable* are their comments?
- Consider the comment itself. Is it *constructive or destructive*?
- It is very helpful to discuss what was said with someone we respect and trust. What is their opinion?

In comments such as, 'You will never amount to anything', the criticism is both negative and demeaning. It is really of no value to us and should be rejected out of hand. It does not help us to understand our weaknesses, nor does it suggest a way that we may improve. But sorting out fact from fiction in what others say about us is usually not so simple.

Take, for example, the verbal abuse of a boy when he was ten years old. He had high artistic and academic abilities and, because of this, other boys in his class called him a 'sissy' on a regular basis. Going to secondary school he was separated from all these boys but their words were deeply embedded. He vowed to himself that he would never be called a sissy again. He gave up anything that was artistic and committed himself to football and cricket, though deep down he did not enjoy sports. Meanwhile the other boys had long forgotten and moved on, but he was still affected (attached) to the power of what was said. Those 'power' words and his reaction to them had radically shaped his life.

Reflection on the Scriptures

James 3:1–12

Read these verses and drink in what is being said. James warned about the power of the tongue. In our speech we have the power to build others up and to pull them down, to bless them or to curse them.

- Do you receive 'mixed' or confusing messages from anyone close to you?
- Are you inclined to give 'mixed' messages or critical words to some people whom you meet regularly?
- What impact does this have on your relationships with them?
- Is there a better and wiser way to be found in the letter of James?

For meditation and discussion

- Can you recall a point in your life where a negative experience or event resulted in you feeling 'stuck' or trapped?
- In practical terms, how can you begin to put behind you the negative words and actions of others?

The following material can be used either as **preparation for Week 4**, or, should your group be taking six weeks over this study, as **Week 5**.

PRACTICAL STEPS TO FINDING FORGIVENESS WHEN I AM THE OFFENDER

STEP 1: Affirm the biblical truth that God is loving, understanding and forgiving

STEP 2: Acknowledge the offence to yourself – be specific

- Face up to exactly what you have done and own up to whom you have hurt in the process.

STEP 3: Confess to God and another trusted person – be specific and completely honest

- Guard against the tendency to excuse yourself by partly blaming others. Simply own *only* your contribution to the offence, even if you believe others were also at fault.
- This disclosure should also be made to the person offended if they are aware of the offence.
- Usually it is not appropriate to 'dump' *new* information on the person against whom one has offended, for example, 'I want you to know that I have hated you for the last ten years but God has convicted me of this and I have asked His forgiveness. I am sorry.'
- The situation where a spouse has been unfaithful and the other spouse does not appear to know is a different and more difficult circumstance altogether.

STEP 4: Pray for the mercy and grace of God to deal with your personal sin

- He has promised to respond to this prayer (Rom. 5:1–11).

STEP 5: Make restitution if this is relevant

- Pay back money and so on.

STEP 6: Be accountable and transparent with a trusted person of the same sex who is willing and able to see you through the process of starting again

STEP 7: Actively seek reconciliation if this is in the best interests of the offended party

- Where both appropriate and possible, restore relationships, firstly with God, then with others who have been offended by you.
- In cases of a serious offence, this is not appropriate and should not be considered.
- Reconciliation is never guaranteed – it is often an offer we make because, understandably, offended people do not always want to reconcile.
- Sometimes the other person has died or moved to an unknown location.
- Remember, however, that God is always seeking reconciliation with His children. His heart for us is reconciliation – with Himself and with others (see 2 Cor. 5:16–21).

STEP 8: Rebuild trust where appropriate

- The warnings given for reconciliation apply here also.
- Building trust is always a process and usually takes a long time.
- Following some offences, it is inappropriate to expect the level of trust to be restored to where it was before the offence, for example, child abuse, financial crimes, infidelity, untruthfulness.

STEP 9: Live as a forgiven person

Romans 8:1–17
Labelling yourself as a saved sinner is not helpful. The power to go forward is

in the grace of God and the fact that you and I, despite our sins and failures, are His children by His choice.

Colossians 3:1–17
Put in place in your life new, biblical, helpful ways of thinking, behaving and choosing,

- concerning God
- concerning self
- concerning others

This requires a deliberate moving on; not remaining immobilised by the memories and experiences of sin(s) that have been forgiven. This may prove to be quite a struggle!

Remember, this is not a minimisation of the wrongs committed. It is an embracing of the work of the cross of Christ and an application of the forgiveness of Jesus so that we may continue to be transformed into His likeness (2 Cor. 3:7–18).

Forgive! Life is too precious to be consumed by regrets, controlled by rage, or complicated by plans for revenge.

> *To the Jews who had believed him, Jesus said, 'If you hold to my teaching, you are really my disciples. Then you will know the truth, and the truth will set you free.'* John 8:31–32

> *Jesus answered, 'I am the way and the truth and the life. No-one comes to the Father except through me.'* John 14:6

OVERCOMING

◎ 1. TO GROW TO GREATER MATURITY

Every human being suffers at the hands of others. This may be anything from relatively minor offences to gross abuse.

We all suffer pain and some of this can be excruciating at times. The enemy of our souls desires that these offences will humiliate and harm us. Essentially, he wants to undermine the threat we pose to his kingdom by sending trials and temptations our way through other human beings and through circumstances beyond our control.

The epistle of James encourages us to not waste our sorrows and trials (James 1). We have seen in previous weeks how the apostle Paul learned from the variety of good and bad experiences he went through. It was because of the battles that he was able to say,

> I know what it is to be in need, and I know what it is to have plenty. I have learned the secret of being content in any and every situation, whether well fed, or hungry, whether living in plenty or in want. Phil. 4:12

As in Paul's case, with God's help, the intention of the offences will not win through; they will not stop us from loving, forgiving, moving on and growing in our inner person as we journey with God and others.

The day the child realizes that all adults are imperfect, he becomes an adolescent; the day he forgives them, he becomes an adult; the day he forgives himself, he becomes wise. Alden Nowlan

Reflection on the Scriptures

James 1; 1 Peter 1:1–9

Does the statement, 'Consider it pure joy … whenever you face trials of many kinds' (James 1:2), appear just a little unreal to you?

On the surface it certainly could! However, in certain contexts it does make considerable sense. For example, a marathon runner has an intense and difficult training routine, even before the challenge of the event itself. Some potential runners may quit because they cannot endure the training. Suppose that this barrier is overcome; then the challenges of the race itself are even more difficult. Muscle fatigue, dehydration, dropping energy levels and the grinding out of step after step for hours, are all hurdles to be overcome. So why do athletes do it? Because of their individual goals: the prize, the acclaim, the sense of achievement, the money to be won, or perhaps for the sheer satisfaction of meeting the challenges involved. From this point of view, the race is viewed as a means to an end.

In this context the end *does* justify the means – whatever it costs. James views the trials of life very much as the runner views the winning post. The goal for James is maturity. The trials are simply part of the way of developing fitness to reach the goal of personal maturity.

- How do we respond to the statement: 'Don't waste your sorrows?'
- How can we use the hard experiences of our lives to make us stronger, and more mature Christians?

For meditation and discussion

An old ditty ran something like this:

Two men looked through prison bars.
One saw mud, the other stars.

- Do you tend to be a 'mud' or 'stars' person?
- Are you able to use your times of adversity for your benefit, or do such times simply depress you?
- What positive things have you learned from the hard times you have been through?
- Have you grown through hard times or have they simply become a burden to you?

◎ 2. TO BREAK THROUGH IN SEASONS OF TRIAL

Although offences committed against us are very hurtful and harmful, they cannot compare with the offences that we ourselves have committed and that God has completely forgiven us for. When we recognise the amazing fact that God has forgiven us totally and at great cost, we can appreciate the far-reaching influence of His forgiveness. How many people have benefited from His forgiving attitude? However painful offences are in our lives, Jesus suffered more. Yet, at the same time, He showed the way through these seasons of trial.

It is difficult to read and reflect on the biblical characters featured in Hebrews 11 without drawing courage from their faith – faith expressed in so many diverse and difficult circumstances. Yet chapter 12 takes us to a higher level still, culminating in verse 3: 'Consider him [Jesus] who endured such opposition from sinful men, so that you will not grow weary and lose heart.'

Jesus said to His disciples, '... In this world you will have trouble. But take heart! I have overcome the world' (John 16:33).

Reflection on the Scriptures

Romans 8:18–39

Offences are very personal events. We may feel suddenly isolated from the rest of the world as we seek to understand and come to terms with what has occurred. It is certainly true that no one else has been through what we have been through. And they do not know how we feel, no matter what sympathetic people may say.

A most encouraging thought for the Christian is found in this magnificent passage. No matter what the nature of the pain, no matter how intense it may be, no matter how long it may last, God *never* leaves us! *Nothing* separates from His love! We are *not alone*!

- As you meditate on this passage, which of the various trials listed is most like your situation right now?
- In the tough times you've been through, have you ever been aware of the love of God coming to you through the words and actions of others?

For meditation and discussion

The bombing of Coventry Cathedral in 1940 confronted Christians with a difficult forgiveness situation. From the burnt-out shell, two crosses were framed – one from wood and one from nails.[2]

There is a hard law, that when a deep injury is done to us, we never recover until we forgive. Alan Paton

- Have you crossed all the bridges of forgiveness that you have faced?
- If not, what do you plan to do about those that remain uncrossed?
- Do you need support or prayer from others in order to take the first steps?

Practical steps towards forgiveness ... how to cross the bridge
With God, His mercy always has a priority over His justice (James 2:12–13). The New Testament is quite clear in its teaching that God expects His people to have the same forgiving and merciful attitude towards others. Forgiveness is costly!

On pages 21–24, practical suggestions are offered to help each of us move forwards across the bridge of forgiveness of others. On pages 31–33 we look at how to receive forgiveness ourselves.

Closing thoughts

Forgive and forget is a nice thought but most unrealistic, except perhaps in the case of very minor offences. For the most part, the painful memories, shrouded and distorted perhaps by time, will live on in our thoughts, our feelings, and in some circumstances within our bodies.

Remember that the wounds Jesus suffered on the cross were still visible after His glorious resurrection! He understands. Nothing can separate us from His love!

Notes

[1] Corrie Ten Boom, *The Hiding Place* (London: Bantam, reissue edition 1984).

[2] David Douglas, *Coventry Cathedral's Message of Forgiveness*, article available online at www.religion-online.org

OTHER RESOURCES FROM CWR...

Life Issues for Homegroups: Relationships

People long for meaningful relationships – and this is exactly what we see portrayed in the Godhead and in His creative plan. The aim of this group study by Lynn Penson is to look at what He reveals about Himself and about His plan in creating us. In this way, we can understand how we can better relate to our boss, our children, our colleagues, our church family and the many other people we interact with.

£2.99
ISBN: 978-1-85345-447-9

We currently have seven daily dated Bible reading notes. These aim to encourage people of all ages to meet with God regularly in His Word and to apply that Word to their everyday lives and relationships.

Every Day with Jesus – devotional readings for adults. ISSN: 0967-1889
Inspiring Women Every Day – for women. ISSN: 1478-050X
Lucas on Life Every Day – life-application notes. ISSN: 1744-0122
Cover to Cover Every Day – deeper biblical understanding. ISSN: 1744-0114
Mettle – for 14–18s. ISSN: 1747-1974
YP's – for 11–15s. ISSN: 1365-5841
Topz – for 7–11s. ISSN: 0967-1307

£2.25 each per bimonthly issue (except *Mettle*: £3.99 per four-month issue).

Get the benefit of Insight

The *Waverley Abbey Insight Series* gives practical and biblical explorations of common problems, valuable both for sufferers and for carers. These books, sourced from material first presented at Insight Days by CWR at Waverley Abbey House, offer clear insight, teaching and help on a growing range of subjects and issues.

Self-esteem: 978-1-85345-409-7   **Bereavement:** 978-1-85345-385-4
Eating Disorders: 978-1-85345-410-3   **Anxiety:** 978-1-85345-436-3
Stress: 978-1-85345-384-7   **Anger:** 978-1-85345-437-0

£7.50 each

Courses from CWR

We run a range of biblically-based training courses at our headquarters of Waverley Abbey House, Farnham, Surrey, England. These include courses on counselling and on life issues such as forgiveness.

For more details, call our Training Department on **+44 (0)1252 784700** or visit our website: **www.cwr.org.uk**

Prices correct at time of going to print.